FIRST SIGHT

POLAR ANIMALS

Lionel Bender

GLOUCESTER PRESS
London · New York · Toronto · Sydney

Introduction

The areas around the North and South Poles are covered in ice, snow and cold water. The climate there is bleak and hostile. Even in summer the temperature only rises to about 8°C above freezing, and in winter it can fall to 70°C below. Yet many animals live in these regions. Most species have a thick coat or a layer of fat to protect them from the cold. Some animals spend the coldest months asleep in dens beneath the snow. Others are just summer visitors.

All polar animals depend on the plants that grow in the seas or on the land during the summer. Some, such as seals, feed in the water but still rest and breed on the shore. Here many of them are killed and eaten by land animals like Polar Bears and Arctic Foxes.

Contents

◁ **The Musk-ox has a coat of dense soft wool and thick hair**

North and south

The two polar regions are at opposite ends of the Earth. The northern region is known as the Arctic, and the southern region, the Antarctic. The Arctic is an area of frozen ocean surrounded by large masses of land. Animals such as the Caribou, Musk-ox and Arctic Hare live there. They all feed on land plants, and are a source of food for meat-eaters like the Polar Bear and the Wolf. The Beluga, Narwhal, Walrus and several species of seal live in the cold Arctic seas.

The Antarctic is a mass of land permanently buried beneath a great sheet of ice. In this polar region the biggest land animals are insects! But the world's largest animal, the Blue Whale, lives in the icy waters. Huge populations of penguins, sea lions and fur seals also feed along the edge of the ice sheet.

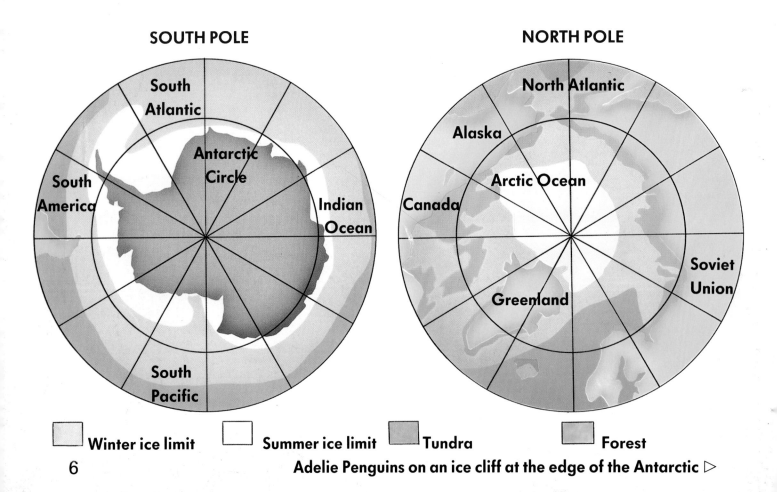

SOUTH POLE   **NORTH POLE**

South Atlantic

Antarctic Circle

South America

Indian Ocean

South Pacific

North Atlantic

Alaska

Arctic Ocean

Canada

Soviet Union

Greenland

Winter ice limit   Summer ice limit   Tundra   Forest

   Adelie Penguins on an ice cliff at the edge of the Antarctic ▷

Polar Bears

The Polar Bear is the largest and strongest hunter in the Arctic. A fully grown male may measure 2.7m (9ft) in length and weigh 450kg (1,000lb). The bear's favourite food is seals, which it stuns with a blow from one of its huge front paws and then tears apart with its teeth and claws. But Polar Bears also eat fish, birds and their eggs, and scraps of food thrown away by people.

In October, as winter approaches, a pregnant female Polar Bear carves out a den deep in the snow. She spends the cold months here, giving birth to her cubs in December. The newborn cubs feed on mother's milk until they are six months old. All the bears leave the den in March or April. Soon after, the young start to eat meat.

Polar Bears are good swimmers. When they go into icy cold waters, their thick, oily fur and a layer of fat beneath the skin keep them warm. They paddle with their front legs and use their hind legs as a rudder to steer. Polar Bears can swim steadily for many hours to get from one ice floe to another.

Polar Bear swimming

Cross-section of a Polar Bear den

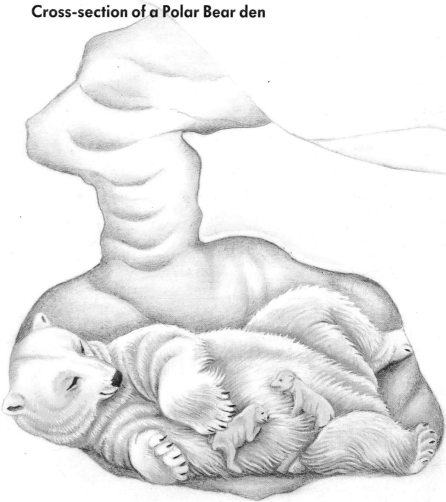

◁ **A Polar Bear mother and her two cubs venture across the ice**

Predators and prey

Some Arctic meat-eaters such as the Wolf and Lynx are predators – they hunt and kill other animals. The animals they hunt, called their prey, range from Reindeer and Musk-ox to Arctic Hare and Lemmings. Other meat-eaters like the Wolverine (also called the Glutton) are scavengers. They steal the kills of predators and feed on any dead animals they find.

Birds of prey such as the Golden Eagle and the Snowy Owl hunt from the air. They feed on small mammals and birds that live and breed in the far north. The birds fly low over the ground in search of food, swooping down to catch and kill animals with their talons. They rip their prey apart with their hooked beaks.

Musk-oxen grouped together to protect themselves from a pack of wolves

Musk-oxen are easy prey for hunters as they do not run away when attacked. Instead, the adults form a protective circle, keeping their young in the middle and facing outwards.

A Wolverine defends its food and territory aggressively

A Golden Eagle stands guard over a dead deer

Male Walruses fighting

Life on the ice

Walruses live on ice floes, sometimes far out to sea. They spend a lot of time in the water, ploughing the seabed with their long upper teeth, or tusks, for clams. They eat the flesh of these animals after sucking it from the shells with their thick, muscular lips. When they are not feeding, Walruses rest or sleep on ice floes or beaches. To haul themselves out of the water, they dig their tusks into the ice and "walk on their teeth" until safely ashore. Walruses also use their tusks as weapons against predators such as Killer Whales, or to keep open a breathing hole in the ice.

Like all penguins, the Adelie Penguin is a flightless bird that lives in the Antarctic. It uses its wings as paddles and to help it leap up onto ice floes. Adelie Penguins feed on tiny animals called krill.

Walruses "walking on their teeth"

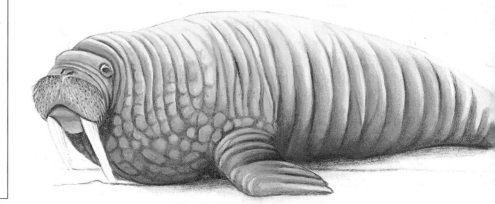

◁ **Gentoo Penguins wandering in the Antartic snowscape**

13

Under the snow and ice

Baby Ringed Seals are born in April in snow caves hollowed out by their mothers. The snow keeps the young seals safe from predators such as Arctic Foxes and Polar Bears. It also keeps the seals warm until they have developed a thick insulating layer of fat, or blubber. At first their coat is white. But by the time they are one month old it has taken on a grey, blotchy look. The rings on the coat that gave the seals their name become more distinct as they get older.

Ringed Seals are found throughout the Arctic. They feed on fish and shelled animals like shrimp and crabs. Like all seals, they have to come to the surface of the water to breathe. When the seas freeze over, they scratch and butt at the ice to make air holes.

The Narwhal lives among drifting ice floes in the Arctic Ocean. Males develop a slender tusk up to 3.3m (10 ft) long.

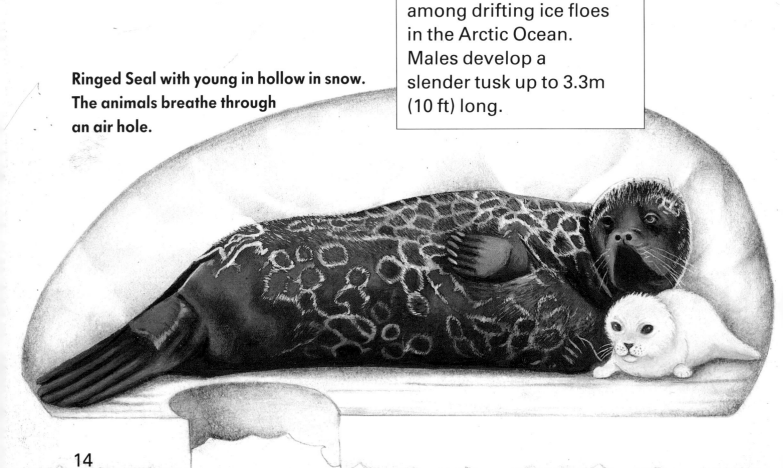

Ringed Seal with young in hollow in snow. The animals breathe through an air hole.

Wilson's Petrel feeding on plankton

King Eider Duck

Food from the water

In the summer, the Arctic and Antarctic seas teem with life. Tiny plants, the phytoplankton, drift in the water. These plants are the main food for animals such as krill, which look like tiny shrimp. Krill are eaten in huge quantities by whales, seals, fish and seabirds.

The treeless Arctic landscape, called the tundra, is also home to many animals. The tundra contains thousands of lakes, marshes, mudflats and estuaries. In the spring, these watery areas are filled with weeds, algae, insect larvae and fish. This aquatic life is a source of food for birds like ducks, geese, swans and divers. Most of these birds breed and nest on the tundra.

The Humpback Whale filters small animals such as krill from the Arctic waters. It does this with the sieve-like plates, called baleen plates, that hang down on either side of its mouth. For this reason it is known as a baleen whale.

Loon diving for fish

◁ **A Humpback Whale "breaching", leaping out of the water**

At the water's edge

For Southern Elephant seals, September and October are the busiest months of the year. This is the start of the Antarctic spring when the seals come ashore to breed. The males land first and battle with one another for areas of the beach. The females follow a few weeks later. They gather in groups around the winning males. Pups from the last year's mating are soon born and their mothers mate again a week or so later.

In the spring, water birds nest and breed in their millions along the edges of Arctic lakes. Bewick's Swans build a mound of water plants up to 3m (10ft) across. Canada Geese lay their eggs in hollows lined with leaves, grass and down that they pluck from their own breasts.

A nesting Bewick's Swans with its young, or "cygnet"

Young male Elephant Seals in a playful contest ▷

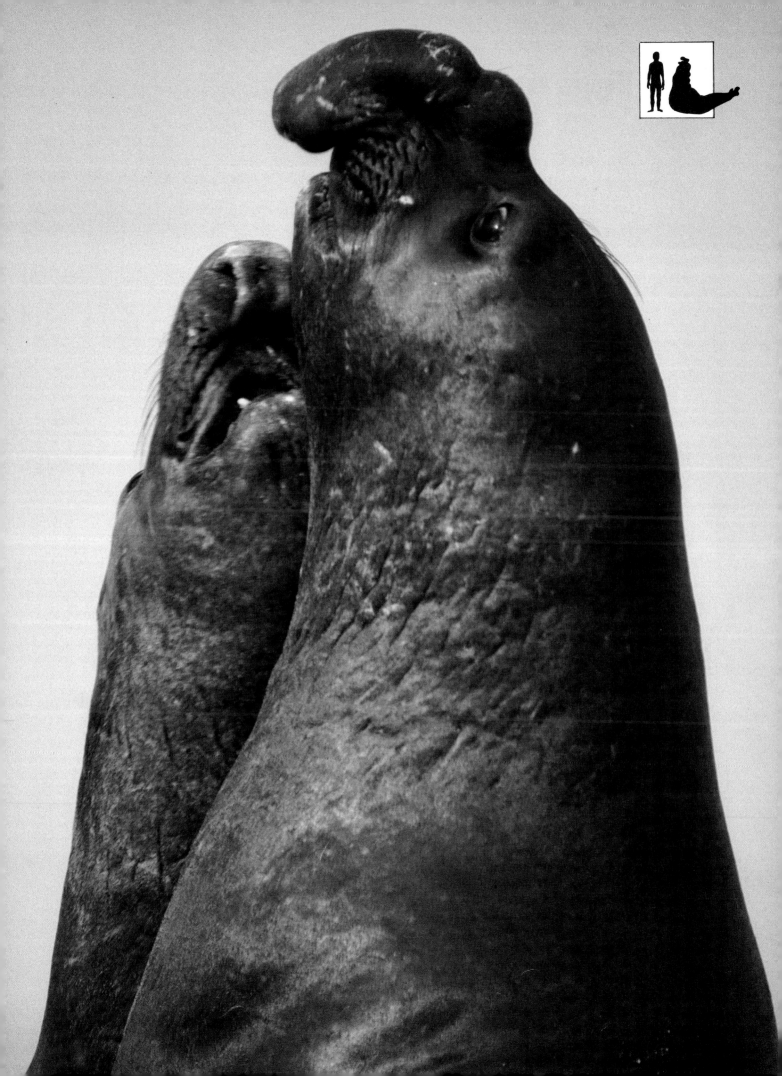

Eggs and young

Female Emperor Penguins lay a single egg, which they carry on their feet. They cover the egg with a fold of skin to keep it warm. After a few days, the fathers take over incubating the eggs and the mothers waddle off across the ice to feed in the water. They return eight weeks later, just as hatching starts, with their stomachs full of partly-digested fish and squid.

The mother penguins feed the chicks while the hungry males go off to feed themselves. The chicks venture into the water in December, when food is most plentiful in the Antarctic. By the time they are fully grown the Emperor Penguins will stand almost 1m (3ft) tall and weigh 45kg (100lb).

Emperor Penguin with chick

Arctic Terns nest in the far north. Both parents look after the chicks, which are born fully-feathered and can swim when only a few days old. The main food of Arctic Terns is fish. The birds hover just above the ocean's surface, then dive into the water and grasp their prey in their beaks. Arctic Terns spend one summer in the Arctic and the next in the Antarctic – six months later.

An Arctic Tern looks after its newborn chick ▷

Colour changes

The Rock Ptarmigan is a bird that lives in the tundra and mountains of the north. It feeds on Arctic plants, and is eaten by foxes and birds of prey. In the summer the bird's plumage is mottled brown, which blends in well with surrounding rocks and lichens. In the autumn, its colouring gradually changes to pure white. This protects the Rock Ptarmigan from predators by making it difficult to see against the snow.

The Arctic Hare and Arctic Fox also change colour with the seasons. Both have a greyish-brown summer coat and a white winter coat. But while the hare's winter colouring helps it to escape predators, the fox's allows it to stay concealed while it hunts other animals.

Stoat in summer

The Stoat is an Arctic predator that has two coats – and two names. In the autumn, its red-brown fur changes to white. The animal is then called an Ermine.

Ermine in winter

The Rock Ptarmigan's winter plumage blends in with the snow...

...while its summer feathers are the colour of the tundra rocks and plants   23

Migrations

As summer approachs, many birds and mammals travel great distances to the polar regions. They go to feed on the plants that burst into growth as the long warm days begin. In Canada, huge herds of Caribou migrate 1,000km (600 miles) or more to the Arctic tundra. Their young are born in June. In August, as winter draws near, the whole herd starts the journey south to the forests where they will spend the winter.

In the Antartic, seabirds like albatrosses, gulls and petrels constantly roam the seas. They feed on the fish, krill and squid that live in the huge southern oceans. Wandering Albatrosses may spend several years at sea. The adult birds travel once or twice around the vast ice cap before coming ashore to breed.

Lemmings live in the far north of Canada, Scandinavia and Siberia. In the winter they live in tunnels beneath the snow. They mainly breed in the summer. Every three or four years their populations become too large for the food supply. When this happens, groups of thousands of lemmings migrate together to find new homes and sources of food. Many of them die on the way.

Norwegian Lemmings on the move

Migrating Caribou herds can contain up to 50,000 animals ▷

Insects

Insects thrive during the short polar summers. In the Antarctic they live on the few plants that grow in sunny, sheltered places. Water Beetles and Mosquito larvae live in Arctic pools and lakes. Mosquitoes are a major pest to some mammals. Huge swarms of them follow the Caribou herds, feeding on the animals' blood.

Insects called Springtails have survived in Arctic ice for as long as three years. Other insects contain an anti-freeze which prevents the liquids in their bodies from turning to ice in the winter. But most polar insects hibernate, or pass the winter in a resting stage. They become active again as soon as the snows melt.

A female Mosquito on a tundra rock

26

A Small Copper Butterfly sucks nectar from an Arctic flower ▷

Survival file

People have lived in the Arctic region for thousands of years. The best-known are the Eskimos, or Inuit, of North America and Greenland, and the Lapps of northern Scandinavia and the Soviet Union. The Inuit hunt seals and whales to eat, but only kill as many as they need to support themselves. Some Inuit and Indians also still follow the migrating Caribou herds. In the past, they moved with the herds on sledges pulled by Husky Dogs. Today, many Inuit use motorised sledges or snowmobiles. The Lapps look after tame herds of Reindeer, another name for Caribou. They rely on these animals for food (milk, cheese and meat), transport and clothing.

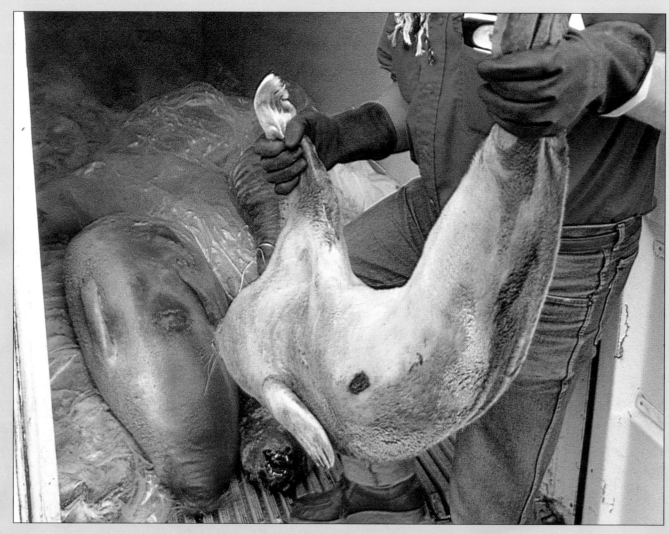

These diseased seals were found washed up on a Danish beach

The Antartic was not inhabited until the 1800s. At that time explorers, and later whalers and fur trappers, began to arrive. Since then, the wildlife in both polar regions has been seriously threatened by man. Most species of whales have been hunted almost to extinction for their blubber, meat and oils. Seals, Polar Bears, Arctic Foxes and Stoats have all been killed for their fur. Walruses and Narwhals were hunted for their ivory tusks.

A Lapp with his Reindeer herd

Both polar regions have been badly damaged and polluted in the last hundred years. This has happened because of oil and mineral exploration, the construction of roads and airstrips, and the use of vehicles that can travel over snow and ice. Oil spills, like the huge one caused by a tanker accident in Alaska in the spring of 1989, are especially destructive. The plant life, and the animal life that depends on it, have been permanently upset.

This gannet was killed by oil pollution

Fortunately, a lot of the commercial activity in the Arctic and Antarctic is being controlled. The countries responsible for developing the two polar regions have signed various treaties and agreements. There are now international laws that restrict the hunting of many polar animals to certain numbers each year. Other laws limit mineral exploration and building to areas where they will not disrupt the environment, and thus the wildlife, too greatly.

Freeing Grey Whales in Alaska

Identification chart

This chart shows you many of the polar animals described in this book, along with a few others you are likely to read about elsewhere. To see most of them you will have to go to a zoo. Each square of the large grid represents 50cm (20in) and of the small grid 2m (6.5ft).

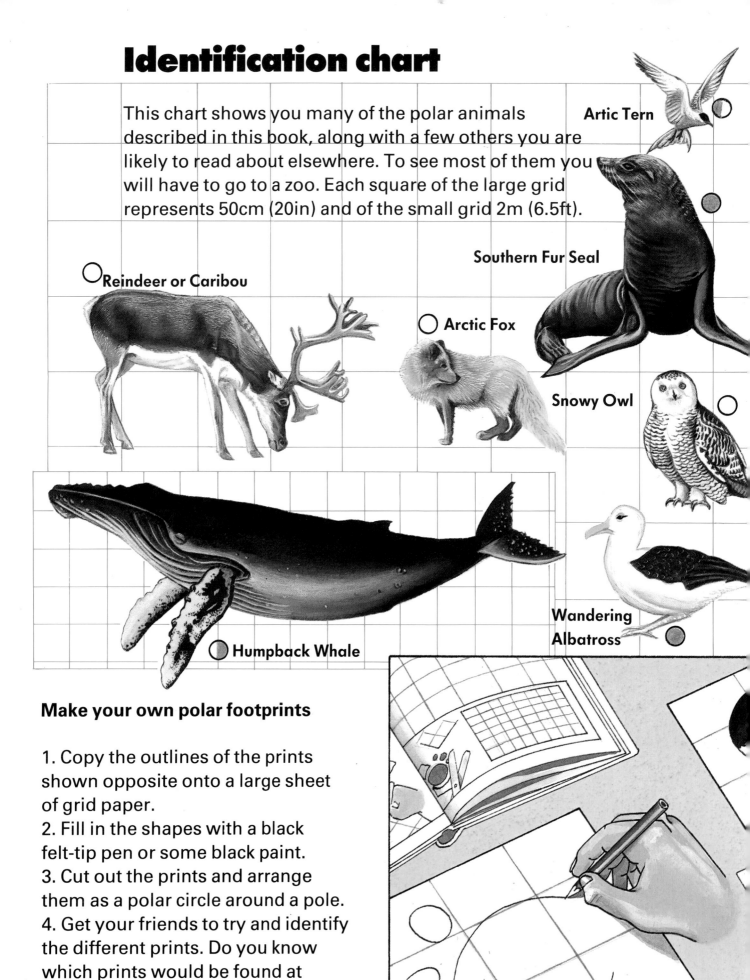

Artic Tern

Southern Fur Seal

Reindeer or Caribou

Arctic Fox

Snowy Owl

Wandering Albatross

Humpback Whale

Make your own polar footprints

1. Copy the outlines of the prints shown opposite onto a large sheet of grid paper.
2. Fill in the shapes with a black felt-tip pen or some black paint.
3. Cut out the prints and arrange them as a polar circle around a pole.
4. Get your friends to try and identify the different prints. Do you know which prints would be found at which pole?

○ Polar Bear

○ Musk-ox

Arctic Hare

● Adelie Penguin

○ Puffin

● Emperor Penguin

○ Walrus

Penguin   Ermine   Snowshoe Hare

The Pole

Polar Bear

Arctic Fox

Seal

Musk-ox   Goose

Index

Photographic Credits:
Cover: Survival Anglia;
title page and pages 4,
7, 11 both, 18, 19, 21, 23
both, 25, 26 and 29 top:

Bruce Coleman; pages
8 and 15: Bryan and
Cherry Alexander;
pages 12, 16 and 27;

Planet Earth; pages 28
and 29 bottom: Frank
Spooner Agency; page
29 middle Ardea.

PRINTED IN BELGIUM BY
proost
INTERNATIONAL BOOK PRODUCTION